Infinite Earths

SAMSON BROWN
(Pseudonym for Jamison Slade)

PAGE PUBLISHING
Conneaut Lake, PA

First originally published by Page Publishing 2024

ISBN 979-8-88960-596-6 (pbk)
ISBN 979-8-88960-604-8 (digital)

Printed in the United States of America

This work is dedicated to the source of my strength, drive, and wherewithal to navigate my time on Earth.

My creator: *God*

Also to my best human friend ever, Benjamin J. Beastly, RIP

I know that if it was me who left this planet, it would be you down here doing exactly what I am doing right now.

Introduction

WELCOME TO SAMSONLAND

From here on out all narration will be italicized like so. As this tour of my psyche progresses, it should serve to alleviate any confusion. We will be starting first with My Words, a collection of entries from my own existence. They will be italicized like so.

The tour will reach its second destination when we stop to witness The Stand-Alones. These counterparts have chosen to sacrifice all for a single cause. I really identify with them. They have no family friends, nothing of any value except their personal goals. If it sounds weird now, wait till you meet some of them.

The third and final leg will take us through the lives of The Returners. These counterparts have multiple entries given over a period of time. This represents the bulk of the tour even though the bulk of the entries I have received over the decades have been stand-alones. The Returners can be stand-alones, but stand-alones cannot be returners. Ponder that. I don't make the rules, that's how it works. Pay attention, you will see it in action.

One more thing. This is the most important rule of the tour. I am not these people. They live in other universes. I can see and hear them. I am basically a recording device that is full. I have to dump it somewhere. If you're on this tour, it's because your mind is naturally conditioned to process this information and its contexts. Thank you for your patience. Keep all limbs in the ride at all times. We're off!

My Words

I'M SORRY

I will never understand why you put up with me
It's as if the very air has the power of corrupting me
The harder I try, the harder it gets
My decisions are split half is legit
Half is counterfeit
My life is in your hands now I used to wish I was dead
Then I would know true freedom
But I was born sentenced to write
This life sentence instead
I have plenty of hope for tomorrow
But none for today
It's just an encore performance of yesterday
I'm just one man no more, no less
Failure doesn't matter because as long as I live
I continue to take the tests
I am so sorry to my life please accept my apologies
Your forgiveness is necessary if I'm to finish these anthologies
This new true philosophy
Turns my memories into my property
You know things that I own enjoy on my own
With the company of loved ones or at home alone
I am way past the roadblocks and the black widow webs
I am full speed ahead like the roadrunner I got circles for legs

3:36 a.m.

I burn alive outside to inside
Inside to outside I burn alive
Continually I survive in a volcano
Deeper I dive I don't want to
People look down at me
Stare point and laugh
All the while I burn alive outside to inside
Inside to outside continually I survive
In a volcano deeper I dive
I don't want to

Darkness suddenly all the light gets swallowed
And I adore the peace that followed
But I still burn alive outside to inside
Inside to outside continually I survive
In a volcano deeper I dive
No one knows how I burn alive
Outside to inside inside to outside
I burn alive continually I survive
In a volcano deeper I dive
I don't want to

The Doorway

There once was a girl that stood at a doorway
It led nowhere a place of no hopes no friends
And no prayers
The archway beckoned for her to enter
And even though I stood right behind her
I could not find her nor remind her
Of what the doorway did to blind her

She stepped through.

Psalms 151 (Acrostic Poem)

1) *All people have heard the mention of the Most Holy's name*
2) *But some refuse to answer instead they look to pass blame*
3) *Christ came to bring life break the chains of spiritual strife*
4) *Denounce the ways of evil prepare the church to be a spotless wife*
5) *Eagerly I serve honored by the privilege*
6) *Frankly I deserve to be kicked to the curb for all my former attacks on the word*
7) *God wanted a knight in shining armor in service to the king*
8) *Heaven sent to wage war until the bells of eternity ring*
9) *I cling to the promises stand firm sprout roots through my boots*
10) *Jesus is my Lord from him I got this holy sword*
11) *King and I yes he ain't Yul Brynner now that Christ is my center I am a perpetual repenter*
12) *Love God with your heart, mind, and soul. Love your neighbor like yourself wisdom worth more than gold*
13) *Mankind an oxymoron should be man blind*
14) *Nine-inch nails were hammered in by the hands of misguided men*
15) *Oh Lord, forgive them they didn't understand*
16) *Power and glory only exist in your hands*
17) *Quiet we need a moment of reflective silence*
18) *Razor sharp is the word when its heard it cuts two ways*
19) *Sing a new song of joy, love, and praise*
20) *To the King of Kings the ruler of always*
21) *Useless religion and philosophy got some walking the wrong steps*
22) *Victory lane is patrolled by diehard spiritual vets*
23) *Wages of sin is death and it's a lot of folks dying to get that last check*
24) *X-ray vision I see through fake people and the evil schemes*
25) *Yet and still his burden is lighter than coffee with extra creme*
26) *Zion God's holy mountain I saw us all there once in a dream*

Voices

Can you hear them? If you can't, then how do you know I shouldn't fear
    them
Doctors say that it's all in my head, the Voices are calling me dead
Got a bunch of poison pills the doctors are calling them meds
I sleep most of the day now
Don't socialize much it's like I'm fading away now
Always feeling something ain't right the screws ain't tight
A darkness fight so deep you can't illuminate with a spotlight
Honest shame for carrying blame placed on me
By a nonexistent disembodied Voice with a first name

The Stand Alones

FOLLOW ME

This young man committed suicide. He and his girlfriend made a suicide pact. He went through, and she didn't. This was his suicide note:

It was once said that my hand was held by the divine
Your hand was clenched tightly in the other one of mine
Follow Me
I saw a road that last through each of our pasts
Forks at the presents and dead ends at the future
Follow Me
You hesitated I patiently waited destinies pull is too strong
The sweat from our palms dripped when our grips slipped
Then I blinked and you were gone
Follow Me

The Mural

This counterpart is a world renown artist. His paintings are considered modern-day classics. If it has his signature anywhere on it, it's priceless. His favorite piece was a commissioned piece, a mural on the wall of a new airport. This is what was in his mind as he painted what would eventually become his most publicly hated piece.

Almighty one! Put your foot on the planet shake loose lime-
    stone and granite
Put bedrock in a headlock rip out two-stone tablets
That reminds us of your original Ten Commandments
These people can't stand it that you've raised a knight
Who will fight them all if need be single-handed
Pour on the plagues until the world begs
We paint the town with horrible crimes and murderous
    bloodsheds
Why wait with the earthquakes I dare you break the Richter
    scale
At the same time knockin' down bars and state stores decreasing
    liquor sales
Make it rain Bibles with pages of glass and covers of stone
That hit the ground shatter into shrapnel or hit us on the dome
    and split skull bones
Never again to flood the whole Earth? Well how about a solar
    flare so big…it's a fiery curse
These people need something to see to believe
That's why so many are designed to be deceived

The Sandwich Board

This is one of the most impressive of the stand-alones. He is homeless. He has no earthly possessions other than the clothes on his back and a sandwich board sign. This guy stands in front of his world's White House wearing his sign, yelling the message written on it. Twelve hours a day three hundred. sixty-five days a year. And he has done this for twenty years. This is what is on the sign.

I will sweep away everything in your land says the *Lord*
I will sweep away both people and animals alike
Even the birds of the air and the fish of the sea will die
I will reduce the wicked into heaps of rubble
Along with rest of humanity says the *Lord*
That terrible day of the *Lord* is near swiftly it comes
A day when strong men will cry bitterly
A day when the *Lord's* anger will be poured out
It is a day of distress anguish a day of ruin and desolation

Darkness and gloom black clouds trumpets
And battle cries down go the walled cities and strongest
     battlements
Because you have sinned against the *Lord* I will make you as
     helpless
As a blind man searching for a path
Your blood will be poured out into the dust
And your bodies will lie there rotting on the ground
Your silver and gold will be useless to you on that day
The whole land will be devoured by the fear of his jealousy
He will make a terrifying end to all the people of Earth

*imagine being outside twelve hours each day
Three hundred sixty-five days a year saying that over and over
    again. Some say he's crazy.
He ain't. He's a Stand Alone.

I Have Yet to See Your Face

A couple of recurring themes you will notice on the tour are faith and love.

The counterparts are tortured souls; you have to understand that we all have similar mindsets. You would find the same if you could witness your counterparts. Hard lives make hard people. Soft lives make soft people. Every version of me everywhere has had a hard life.

This guy here never gave up on love. That is his single purpose. Find true love. I know it sounds really corny. But to each his own.

Although I have yet to see your face I've placed
A life with you on layaway I eagerly await
Hopefully it's just a day away and I pray I'm not prey
For the wrong type of woman I wear my heart on my sleeve
So sometimes I won't see the wicked ones coming
I hope there is space in her life for the idea of us
Or is this another clay fantasy miry and useless slush
Maybe I should hush let the orchestrator the composer of time
Alleviate the fears and doubts that exist in our minds
I am crazy for you and have yet to see your face
Or heard your voice with my ears except once
In another universe another time and place
I know I love you as much here as I did there
That's why I won't let you go I must persevere

The Heart Condition

This counterpart is still a child. He asks his single mother why a lot.

One of his many inquiries: Why does God let bad things happen to good people? You've asked it before I have to. His mother's answer is what launches him on his road to being a stand-alone.

There is a hole deep in the hearts of people
And from that explodes all manner of violence and evil
Capillaries and veins swell with black poison
Streaming from our hearts to our brains
We are living beings whose perceptions are so limited
The last thing we should be believing is what our eyes are seeing
We use that to make solutions from excuses that's called human
    reason
Often the blame for our despicable acts
Can be placed on our media and cherry pickable facts
When it's more like a third ventricle is what our heart lacks
Some say its video games, music, or TV
I can see that but to me that's too easy
This situation has become such an emergency
I think what we need is a type of open heart surgery
It ain't perjury to call *God* the anatomy sheriff
Placing cardiac under arrest
The human heart has been over taxed like the IRS or tariffs

The Heartache

Remember the last entry, the young man whose mother's advice set him on a certain path? Well, this entry came to me the day after his mother's funeral. I seldom get revisits from stand-alones. Enjoy!

Before the throne of the almighty I humbly kneel
Covered in a cloak of guilt forgiveness is my appeal
Been caught up too long by the darkness in my own heart
Now I'm looking for a change I desire a fresh start
The throne was easy to find but hard to approach
The forces of evil deceive you to keep you from getting close
My loved ones have been used as tools
Then the betrayal sets in now I'm their personal fool
They want to enter my life imposing their own rules
But that ain't the case I find them to be drones automatons
The NPC face and I only follow them to discover what they
    chase
The outcomes of the fates weeping and gnashing of teeth
The only sounds heard in that place
But my mom she standing at them pearly gates
I'm trying to get there because to me heaven can't wait

T. R. U. S. T

(THE REASON U STAY THERE)

This stand-alone has dedicated himself to his only son, Solomon. Being a single father has given him a unique perspective on his son. It was why when Solomon got dumped by his first love that his father had this to say.

The reason you stay there stiff like a board you will stand
No wasting by placing faith in man
It's like leaning on a sharp stick
That breaks in the middle and pierces your hand
Look at these folks most of them are insecure jokes
Insane schemes to achieve their dreams
And at the same time peddling false hopes
Give the rope watch them hang themselves
They will tie and put the noose around their own throats
In the end half your friends will prove to be otherwise
They got other lives behind your back
And in your face your mother lies
Everybody needs somebody but that trust needs to be earned
Take it from a guy who has been burned
By friends, family, and females they all had a turn
Relationships will always end over ends, end over men, end over
    friends
And don't forget time the purpose of any relationship of any
    kind
Exists so it can end and nine times out of ten
The one you trust most will fade away like a ghost
When the heat of life makes it hot under the pot
They will leave your heart to crumble like toast
Then your trust in them begins to dry rot

Life's wisdom leads to two things: blessings and lessons
If you fail that's okay you can always have makeup sessions
You need to always be yearning
To always be learning
Then you will always be burning
To keep the pages of your life turning

The Soldier

This counterpart here is a military veteran. He enlisted at eighteen and spent more years as a soldier than he has as an adult. Like all standalones, he has no significant others. Every letter he ever received has been from himself to himself. It was during his nations war on terror that he died in combat. His last unmailed letter was found in his pocket. This is that letter.

Dear Samson,

Let me tell you what I know we run a race like Flo-Jo
And me I'm just a nobody like a hobo
Trained to be a killer murderer upon command
And I need you to understand what that can do to a man
There is no off button or a pause switch
I stuff body bags with tagged toes
And patriotism is what I'm taught to call this
I'm afraid to go home after seeing all this
PTSD from I.E.'s. I'm that GI like joe
And tonight is the night I die on foreign soil

What Is love?

This counterpart is recently divorced at this time. He was an abusive prick. She left. Good for her. This is what he said on his last day of anger management.

I was searching for something pure, real something true
Now I don't have a car abandoned by friends
Creditors and bill collectors make sure I can't meet my ends
So I can't pretend anymore to be something I'm not
Always hungry stomach tied in knots
Can't afford nice clothes anymore
No fancy restaurants no more icy watches on my wrists
I'm no longer in the position to make her fall in love with gifts
I wish I would have known love is priceless
I might just not have introduced her to a tight fist
Back then power was in sex
Because that never took a lot of effort for me to get
Now it's a deeper craving for a connected companionship
But I've been so cruel to women all the good ones have yelled
    abandon ship
It eludes me love has become a fevered dream
Of a princess and a redeemed knight in a world overrun with
    sorcerous queens
Women with dark hearts practiced and perfected by the dark
    arts
On a mission of revenge against the abuse of an ex-boyfriend
And now in her mind all men have played a part
Emotions stay on guard because of another immature male
And his lack of regard, what used to be cottony soft is now
    concrete hard
When you find it hold it, time can help shape and mold it

But it takes two to make it work no one can control it
It creates and destroys brings infinite joy
Me? I played with it for a minute like a kid with new Christmas
        toys
Lord knows back then I didn't know what it was
Now I understand all the pain I caused trying to answer
                    What is love?

Utopia

He is in a coma. He fell off a garage when he was thirteen years old. That was about a year ago. He will soon be awake with the most amazing story. It's long but worth it.

Man, where am I? My eyes raise open sunlight blinds me
Then I'm on the gaze scoping I'm hoping I'm somewhere
    familiar
The streets are gold and skyscrapers doesn't even describe these
    buildings
I don't see any bums no projects or slums
This place ain't nothing like the world I'm from
All I can hear is joyous laughter from people in white robes
I see my wife my crew my daughter is there too
This ain't a dream somehow I know all this is true
Is this the promised land that was pledged to an honest man
I'm walking slowly nobody here seems to know me
But everybody is super friendly so I don't feel lonely
People invite me into their homes without knowing my name
My intentions financial positions or from whence I came
We drink milk eat lamb cheese and unleavened bread
Across from me sits my two mothers both of which are dead
Next to them sits a man who claims to be my dad
I welcome him with open arms I ain't even mad
I'm confused normally sharp is the mentals
I can outthink most problems but this ain't that simple
I ask my birth mother please explain this to me
She says you were brought here so that you can see
The place that awaits every country and state
Some ain't making it. That's why it's called the human race
Don't lose that's a horrendous fate

I'm viewing visions of bodies floating in fiery lakes
This scene is too much for my mortal senses to take
I pass out from the strain and when I awake
I see a throne surrounded by smaller versions of the same
A voice from everywhere calls my name
Whoa who is it? But I already know
I drop to my knees fear lives in the sounds
Arise and be recognized before me Samson Brown
The Earth belongs to me for I am the *Lord*
Mankind is the tenant and the rent is to follow my word
That's no too much to ask do you think so my son
I'm the wrong one to ask with all the dirt I done

Utopia (Continued)

This is not part 2, it's a continuation. This was done simply for length management of a single entry.

He says all was forgiven when my blood was shed on the cross
And you will change your direction so you will be no longer lost
I ask him why do you let a world like this continue to exist?
He says even though I know every name on it
The roll call to heaven is a man-made list
My children tend to think it is I who owe
But that debt is already paid so I ask you what are they waiting
    for
Humans must take the first step toward me
Everyone has a place of belonging with me
Men measure success with expensive pleasure and fancy dress
I look at your heart and where I am in it. Pretty much nothing
    else
You have been chosen and I know you will succeed
Because from the fruit of evil you no longer feed
He tells me my lifelong cries have been heard
Me? I'm kind of disturbed I can't even use the phone at home
No one has any time for my words
It matters not he says damnation must be revealed has a choice
And I can see the sincerity as it rolls off his voice
He says it's time for us to part you have seen all I will show
I break down and start crying I just don't want to go
Man where am I as my eyes raise open
Sunlight blinds me for a minute then I'm on the gaze scoping
And for the author writing this alone in his home
Place this entry at the end of The Stand-Alones

The Returners

WATER (PART 1)

Introducing the returners. This series of counterparts have sent multiple entries.
The pattern is usually one event over multiple entries. And yes to whoever asked that,
a returner can be a stand-alone. It's rare, but it has happened.
This here started over a weekend in the mid-nineties by Lake Erie in Cleveland, Ohio.
I was sitting down by the lake on a sunny afternoon when I noticed a major disturbance
in the water just offshore in front of me a watery counterpart stared at me
And as we made eye contact, this is what I heard in my mind.

I can erode mountains harness the life in me through fountains
Old faithful is my name I'm guaranteed to be spouting
All life requires me and I put out fires easily
I once covered the face of the Earth destroying all humanity
Hear the thunder sound I fall from the sky and permeate the underground
In my murky depths lurk sunken cities countless people who took water breaths
Now all subject to watery deaths
It's more life alive in me than you will ever know
I can be crystalized into unique individual flakes of snow
Or I can be frozen into a ship sinking ice flow
What's my name? Is it the same as rain? Aqua H2O the reservoir filler cascade spiller
Spinning down a drain?
Strong enough to rust metal gentle enough to bloom rose petals

Enough pressure to crush and implode
The unprepared who dare to go too far under my sea levels
I turn dirt into mud flash flood and with soap becomes suds
To clean your body and wash the dirt off your duds
I can't support air it surfaces up in me as bubbles
And I love when your children play in me when I'm puddles
Listen to me when I fall from the clouds
They pull me up out the ocean so I can fall back down
My attitude ranges from calm and serene
To incredibly violent, vengeful, terrible know what I mean?
I'm water

Water (Part 2)

I was simply amazed by what I witnessed. I knew if I went back, he would too.

This was years before my diagnosis. I was still living in the pit of denial.

That was dug for me when I was a child.

Soon after I returned to the same bench, he returned too, and this is what he gave me.

I got extremes temperatures use me for the scales
And measurements numbered on how much of me can fit in a
    pail
You can find me in wells and you can find whales in me
I'm crystal clear when I'm fresh and can burn eyes when I'm
    salty
Liquid Switzerland naturally neutral sometimes stagnate
Or full of human pollution and I conform
To whatever container shape you using
I play well with others and I don't mind
I'm a major ingredient in everything from lotion to table wine
Name something and I'm in there how about plastics, paper,
    rubber
Sometimes you don't know I'm in there because I'm incognito
    undercover
I conduct electricity like composers do symphonies
But instead of music I make hydroelectric energy
I remember when authority was given to a man
To move me aside so his people could walk on dryland
I followed the command. Because everything is subject to *God's*
    will

And when they made it across you should have seen all the sol-
diers that I killed
I'm water

Water (Part 3)

That Sunday morning, I couldn't get down to the lake fast enough. The water began churning once more. I knew then that I also would not see him again after this. So I was hoping for an epic finale. And he did not disappoint.

Over 70 percent of me covers the Earth's face
Over 70 percent of me makes up the human race
So when you look in the mirror do you see my face
There is a deep bond here between me, you, and the planet
Search with your heart, mind, and spirit to understand it
Heat me up and I boil I make a pretty rainbows when mixed
    with oil
Farmer's work pays off when I'm used consistently in the soil
I've been brought out of rocks engulfed streets for blocks and
    blocks
And I love it when you get baptized even to me it means a lot
The submergence reemergence looking like Christ when he
    resurfaced
Actually one of the best things about me is being used for that
    purpose
So when the sun's heat is no longer a treat
And flesh begins to sizzle who do you take off the bench for a
    quick quench
Drink guzzle dip or drizzle
             I'm water

The Abomination of Desolation (Part 1)

This counterpart was a literal freedom fighter. His world had entered its version of the apocalypse. I was blessed enough to receive two entries from him while I was shoveling snow at my mother's.

The time has come city streets flooded with red rum
Armed soldiers face resistance of mere children with guns
Rebels against the laws of our new constitution
Instilled by a madman through trickery and illusions
Bred confusion loyalty to subterfuge and lies
Got billions duped into getting microchips for the hand
Or retinal scan for the eyes
Ten countries united made the horns of a beast
Ten toes composed of clay and iron the composite statues feet
Chaotic cries from the dried out tear ducts of babies' eyes
There is no solution no privacy just government intrusions
Worldwide civil confusion is the conclusion
Cities are concentration camps with traitors in collusion
We need to stand together against this common enemy
But humans have been divided to conquer since before BC

The Abomination of Desolation (Part 2)

I saw him and his partner (his wife) dying on an open battlefield. They had managed to get in each other's arms; they literally died at the same time. These were his last words before he gave up the ghost.

The ancient dragon has awakened from his slumber
His name is a number the march of his army rumbles like
    thunder
Across the grasslands and tundra
The hands of peace have been removed from all countries
And if you ain't got his mark then you have no money
People are praying for death but if can't be found
Only the strong survive man they were the first to go down
He has more power than any one man should have
Billions have died by his hands while he relaxing in bloodbaths
Abortion is not a choice now it's mandatory
Religion isn't personal selection it's one category
This won't be avoided no matter what we do
This the new holocaust and this time it ain't just Jews
God help us all this the downfall of humanity aka
Our swan song

Help Wanted (Part 1)

This counterpart here is a family man. These three entries represent his prayers and thoughts regarding his wife, his son, and himself. His marriage has been in trouble for a while, and he is trying to save it.

Help her Father the weight of the world is on her shoulders
She's covered and crying out from under avalanching boulders
She's trusted men now I tell her to trust you
Follow me as I follow you and there is nothing we can't do
I hate to see her cry I keep my hands ready to wipe eyes
I'd rather relax and gaze together into the nighttime sky
What did we see in the void of endless space
She saw darkness I saw the loving grace of our Lord and savior's
      face
Pain is its own medication and wounds will heal
I gaze into my love's eyes and devour her stare like a meal
I continually thank *God* for you and baby that's real
If I have to beg you I will face to the ground eyes tear filled
Rivulets and micro lakes from the saltwater spill
Let me help you find *God* honey I know exactly where he at
He's a circle we're in the middle he's all around us that's fact
But if one of us could go and the other had to stay
I would spend one last night with you and in the morning send
      you on your way

Help Wanted (Part 2)

His son was struggling with the identity we want for ourselves vs the identities others in our lives put on us. It's a familiar struggle for us all. For years, I allowed people to project their fears and insecurities on me, because I felt as if I needed their acceptance or approval of the type of man I wanted to be. My father wasn't around. If he was anything like this guy who sent this entry, I would be a different man. This is how I know.

Help him Father he is still young and still so confused
Help him Father he wants to be a winner all he does is lose
I talk with him as much as I can trying to teach him your ways
Right and wrong from your eyes and how to study
Your word it's something we should do every day
He said he would go to church that made me proud
He is advertising help wanted I can hear him clear and loud
I love my son and his mother I wish I could protect them from
    evil
Like a chill air bouncing off warm covers
I can't I'm insignificant boot vs ant
That's what I made this prayer psalm if you will I don't care call
    it a chant
Because within *God* power and victory is found
Not a figure eight of hate infinitely looping around and around
Hold it down for him Lord show him what you show me
That faith in you equals loving arms to hold me
They mold me, shape me, build me, and consecrate me
It's more than going to church but that's a great start
He's my son and like you Lord he lives in my heart
I'm just a dad trying to do the dad's part

Help Wanted (Part 3)

Being a man and a father means something to him. And it should, he has been inundated with all the anti-male sentiment that certain elements of his society propagate. His philosophy is simple. He was born the child of a woman. Now he is the man that God His father has made him. I don't blame him at all. Masculinity isn't toxic any more than femininity. Evil and black-hearted people are just that. Gender does not play a role.

Help me father at this moment I'm tired
Help me father defend me from the assault of these liars
They're relentless trying to keep me on the ground
Lord lift me up like you do all the time when I'm pinned down
I have my family but I feel like I stand alone
A paragon fighting dark armies in a medieval war zone
Help me hold on make my grip like glue
Build me up transform me into your tower of power
Keep me strong and focused so I can fight past the final hour
I need you desperately in fact we all do
That's why I pray in Jesus's name that you answer when I call
    you

Human Achievement (Part 1)

He was a government-employed scientist and a career guy for twenty plus years. He became a whistleblower once he discovered some disturbing information regarding the applications of his work.

It all began with the wheel since then we been rolling downhill
Advancement is only recognized by those making the mills
The big deals investing capital in them cats on the hill
While the common folk are left to beg, borrow, and steal
We got buildings that extend thousands of feet in the air
The Internet peddles everything from silverware to edible
    underwear
Now that I have your attention I need for the country to pay
    attention
This information I have is going to force some decisions
I already chose mine that's why I stand alone in this mission
Whether you love me or hate me don't make a difference
Every person that has ever lived has been our sisters and brothers
With *God* being the father and Earth being the mother
And here we are so modern but can't get past hairstyles and skin
    colors
So the only thing we really achieve is killing each other

What's the source of our pride
Human achievement
What sins we cannot hide
Human achievement
What's the name of your *God*
Human achievement
Now who's believing and who's deceiving

Human Achievement (Part 2)

This is the time his family began to get pressured by outside forces to pressure him into no longer blowing his whistle. He didn't know it at the time, but his family was already compromised to the point of no return.

Everything nowadays is big business
From hospitals to holy houses of religion
A cover charge for church *God* don't want your money
Tithes and offerings should be used to keep ministries up and
    running
Honestly if it's not being used for that reason
I would be worried that in *God's* eyes that might be high treason
Corporations own the prisons and with that comes inmates
Bought from the government who in turn increase our tax rates
Crime is going to be here forever no way to stop it
But do we have to use people suffering to make privately-owned
    profits
Everything that's achieved happens at the expense of something
    else
Even war is treated like a sport but what about the lives where
    the damage is felt
Who is going to give them help us? The us?
Why not it seems we're either backing or attacking I'm expect-
    ing World War III any day between ruling egos Now watch
    has many pay innocent citizens To the governments we all
    expendable anyway

What's the source of our pride
Human Achievement
What sins we cannot hide
Human Achievement

What's the name of your *God*
Human Achievement
Who's believing and who's deceiving

Human Achievement (Part 3)

Unbeknownst to him is wife and family had already struck a deal to silence him in return for generational wealth. After an interview on a national news program, he disappeared on the way home. What happened to him? I don't know. I'd ask his wife and kids. But be careful you might disappear too.

I'm one of the few who helped astronauts go on space trips
Now kids are being taught in schools it was all fake trips
Let's see we crucified Jesus made our own deadly designer diseases
Split atoms just to destroy cities with the energy it releases
Now I'm in a lab making creatures from scratch
we've cloned sheep and cows I'm trying to stop us from being
     in the next batch
We need to stop that that can needs to stay closed
Mark my words the result of that is going to have us running
     like a nose
Rather than make super soldiers you can send me to jail
I'm going to expose all the truth I can maybe it'll tip some scales
They are trying to replace us with demons they have summoned
     from hell
          What's the source of our pride
             Human Achievement
          What sins we cannot hide
             Human Achievement
         What's the name of your *God*
             Human Achievement
        Who's believing and who's deceiving

Well, his world sucks. Cloning people to summon demons in? That's a lot to process. Take a break you might need it after this one.

Beauty Is a Beast (Part 1)

Now these three entries were a first. A female counterpart. Recently divorced, she married young to a guy she was completely incompatible with. It was hard for me in the beginning to believe she was a counterpart. She is super pretty. So yeah without further ado.

Every man that sees her wants her for his own
At all costs even the destruction of his home
She just wants to be left alone she is tired of being owned
She hasn't loved herself in a while it's time for that to grow
To be done with the old begin with the new
What's pissing her off it's like no one wants her too
All the guys and some chicks just want her body then they
    through
But she is a lady with a behavior standard so that ain't gone do
She is searching for meaning and in that observes human beings
Mentally cataloging strengths and weaknesses she's seeing
Some call it manipulation to her it's a practical way of thinking
Her heart is heavy and her choices don't see very clear
But to her credit she is a soldier so she continues to persevere
All she needs is time and space but her aura pulls people back
    to her face
At this time her thoughts are jumbled and sporadic
Confused paranoia and suicide dreams stalk her attic
Where who what when why is there no peace
Because my dear you bear the flawless and beauty is a beast

Beauty Is a Beast (Part 2)

It's always interesting having a window into the lives of these counter-parts, but since this was my first experience from a woman's perspective. this was very, very informative. The second entry was received during her lunch break. She works in the medical field. And no, I don't feel like a peeping tom. It's like looking in a mirror. I just see myself.

It eludes it escapes she refers to deaths embrace
The misery she wishes for it to vanish with no trace
Most of the men around her seem to have been infected
Even those she never expected
Have crossed the line only to get rejected
I know women where attention like this would go straight to
    her head
Causing her to open the legs for the wrong dude
Then she is left with whole bunch of fatherless kids
She is stronger than that she endured
Keep it up even when the way seems unsure
Everyone in her life thinks of nothing but themselves
That's why she decided to put them all on the shelf
When the dust settles she'll pick them up from where she left
If I could tell her this I would but I can't she loves to learn
So hopefully she should be good
If looks can kill then beauty is a beast
Wearing a spiked collar and a leash
Even though its ferocious all it wants is inner peace

Beauty Is a Beast (Part 3)

I always wanted to see her again for curiosity sake, but alas, it was not to be. As this is the last entry I ever received from this counterpart. Not the last female counterpart. Just the last with this one.

They chase her down in droves have accidents on the road
When the best thing for them if they knew just let her go
Her mistakes are hers to make her rules are hers to break
I wish her the best it's obvious we have different paths to take
Round and round it goes the endless search for answers
Makes us spin in circles like the pirouette of a ballet dancer
I can see now the truth and everything it means
The pain an outburst in anger brings
I know her pain by name it's the same
Type that has us crying in the rain
Some even quit altogether and make a home in bad weather
Only time can tell what time will heal
I pity her so much because no one can reveal
The answers she seeks and unpleasant side effect of beauty
I heard it was a beast

Indivisible (Part 1)

Another freedom fighter. His America elected the wrong president,
And it wasn't the guy everyone thought would be a bad president.
This president slowly systematically turned the government against
The people until civil war was unleashed. Two nights, two dreams.
This is the first of both.

Through this kingdom of chaos I march
Brave and true no fear in my heart
Fleeting shadows skitter across the landscape in the dark
The land of my birth is now enslaved to a demon
A selected and elected monster of suffering and scheming
His administration attacked our minds corrupted our spirits
With the hopes to steal souls divide and conquer
Create enmity between the young and the old?
Women vs men? Making enemies of best friends?
Downplaying atrocities we all knew he had his hands in
His followers are tricked their sick morally led astray
And when I stand for the truth I just get pushed away

Indivisible (Part 2)

The second night, the second dream. I wish I knew more on what caused his nation to fall. I think if I knew more I could be more watchful for my own world. It didn't happen overnight. There were patterns and warnings that were missed.

The truth is poison to men like this
That's why he colluded with big tech to create cancel lists
He attacked our amendments babbling on stage
Always confused and senseless
He has empowered enemies held in check for centuries
Now they are watching us commit suicide
While celebrating an impending victory
The message here is clear elections have consequences
Please heed my warnings vote policy not fear
People once said he would make a nice president
Why because he's a harmless old man that once was vice
    president?
He got on TV and called half the country racist
When you check the archival footage
He has a history of remarks that's tasteless
I saw it coming so did many others
One nation no longer under *God* indivisible
No liberty and injustice for all

Pandora's Box (Part 1)

This particular counterpart was a famous Hollywood screenwriter and director. He was highly regarded as a once in a lifetime talent. Never had a box office flop. Until he made the trilogy he always wanted to make. It was his masterpiece. To the critics and mainstream establishment, it was garbage. To the public, it was.

Once upon a time in a place called Paradise
A pair of individuals let's call them husband and wife
Struck a deal with evil they would receive death for life
There was a box completely see through
And they opened it even though they were warned not to
Invisible terrors poured out lust, envy, pride, hate
Just a few of the countless evils that leapt from the crate
They didn't know that one move ushered in a curse
That would affect every human to ever live on earth
But there was a solution already in place when they did it
A certain chain of events needed to happen so it took a minute
Thanks to the original two we're all born torn
Between what was released into the world
And the solution yet to be born

Pandora's Box (Part 2)

He filmed all three of the movies at once although they were never released. It was rumored he was blacklisted, blackballed, and blacked out. It was as if these films were somehow against the law but in secret.

It was a sneak attack a curved dagger pierced the small of his
    back
He fell to both knees no hesitation to roll forward
He saw a man dressed in black
Our hero is only five ten the opponent is ten five
Evil-looking spiked armor with a seven foot sword at his side
The hero is fully equipped holy sword on his hip
Breastplate of righteousness shield of faith he ready for this
Look around the coliseum every seat is filled with him
They all cheering but who they rooting for him
Or the giant named sin to him it's always a giant
Bent on our destruction to some it's a sinkhole with black hole-
    type suction
Over his head in a wide arc the villain swings his blade
Hollow voice from inside his helm yells about the skin he wants
    to flay
He's fast for a big cat, gotta give him that
Shield up to block now it's time for counterattacks
Two swift thrusts to his knees now he can't stand
He let him know with a critical blow
And peeled him out his armor like a can
He's gone now but he'll return evil don't stop
And we all guaranteed to fight it thanks to Pandora's box

Pandora's Box (Part 3)

The Lost Sequel. The one knows one has ever seen. I will do my best to describe what I saw. I only ask that you do your best to find the truth in what this entry brings.

Camera zoom in on a scene on the top of a hill
A crowd gathers around human suffering sales
Panoramic view leads us down to city streets
One lone figure is being pelted with watermelon rinds, lettuce
    heads, and beets
Who is this guy beaten so bad looks like he could die
He dragging a wooden cross looks like twice his size
As I wander through the streets I wonder why
Flashback! Three days before to a deafening roar
People are gathered by the city gates like never before
On the back of a colt walking on a carpet of palms
Some are yelling hosanna! Others are crying with outstretched
    arms
I hear he is a king come to free his people
From a foreign-occupying invading force servants of evil
He is a man of obvious authority and power quite possibly no
    equal
This field trip through time takes us further back
To a cave a young pregnant woman in labor on her back
No surgeon or midwife to help with what's emerging
She should be yelling now…but it's not even hurting
What's weird is after the son is born she still a virgin
How can that be? A baby born to a woman that never knew a
    man?
She was blessed by the spirit of *God* to bring forth
The previously mentioned backup plan

Where Is the Fun in the Game? (Part 1)

The information behind this entry is odd. Apparently this is his life played in reverse three key events that shaped him from the near end to early life. Check it out. I hope you find this one as interesting as I do.

When he first seen her he cared nothing about the girl's
demeanor
And even though he had a wife he still wanted to get between
her legs
So different ideas danced through his heads
To make a long story short they ended up in the bed
He told his friends they gave him props
Told him don't stop but the wife got suspicious he wasn't home
a lot
Around this time the mistress was getting hipped too
She checked his wallet when he slept he should have expected
her to
She found his info now he was in for a lot of pain
The mistress had the missus address and name
When the heat came this guy tried to reverse the blame
He got more lies in his mouth than sharks do teeth
Because of his pursuit of another piece wound up homeless on
the street
The mistress bounced the wife, divorced him, and threw him
out
They ended being girlfriends living in his old house
He got what he deserved but he got much more to catch
Physically he's grown but his mind hasn't caught up to his body
yet

Hell hath no fury like a woman scorned
Feel the flames
Every time he sees his reflection he asks himself
Where is the fun in the game?

Where Is the Fun in the Game? (Part 2)

Part 1 was near the end of his life. This part here is the mid-thirties. I don't like him. Many of the counterparts you have met on this tour have been decent. No dice here, straight villain. This man is evil. Watch what he does here.

Now physically this girl could be a work of art
She was drop-dead gorgeous but cursed with a proud heart
She could get any guy that dare look into her eyes
A man got attracted to her like metal to a magnet completely
    mesmerized
She wanted to be spoiled like milk
Dressed in finery furs cashmere and silks
So much ice on her hands she can teach how igloos are built
She got the guy she wanted local kingpin you know a thug type
    of cat
At first he acted exactly the way she wanted him to act
Then all of a sudden he wasn't the guy she fell in love with
He abused her with his mouth then abused her mouth with a
    gloved fist
He was treating her at this stage like a prisoner of war
His words I can always buy me a bitch or rent me a whore
Strange women start calling her self-esteem been falling
He said he owned her that's why he loaned her out to a crew
A bunch of cutthroat scoundrels with no limits assigned to what
    they could do
I ain't even about tell you all the stuff they put her through
She feels so dirty, nasty, and cheap she no longer eats or sleeps

She so scared of him now she has no courage to leave
She died from a disease called A I Dees
Where is the fun in the game?

Where Is the Fun in the Game? (Part 3)

For him this is where it all began. How, when, and where he chose to become what he became.

Don't feel any pity, sympathy, or compassion for him. He would have none for you. He is evil.

From the time he was young with the wrong crowd this boy
    hung
Financially strapped in the hood so the street life song he sung
He started small time selling dummies to the dummies
Dressed code clean now clothes ain't bummy
Young girls on him hard his pockets are full of blood money
He had gained quite a rep 18 and considered a vet
He had shoot out with cops to him they're no threat
He lived through the gunfire exchange led away locked in chains
15 with an L because he left a cop lying in bloodstains
He was hard on the boulevard in the yard not so much
Lifers smacking his butt calling it a creampuff
He got beat toothless by Big Rufus so now he can't bite
Rippin' through his rectum got him screaming for c.o. all night
Every day for the next x years of his life he lived imprisoned
In a prison of being the prisoner's wife
Where is the fun in the game?

Critical Condition (Part 1)

This man works very hard for his family. He has been blessed with a loving, compatible wife and five kids, two are in college and three are in high school. Because of their hard work, they have provided a decent upbringing (financially at least) for the children. This entry is him leaving work on a Friday evening.

I cross the street at 4:00 on the dot an hour to rest before my
    second shift needs me to hit the clock
7:30 a.m. to 9:30 at night necessary for me to make it
Working is my way of life
I walk past the store and the showgirl bar
On the way some guys flag me down from afar
Can you spare a dollar, quarter, or a nickel
Wino's and fiends nope can't even spare a little
Instead I ask ain't you tired of having nothing at all
Asking for handouts from strangers tell me how did you fall
Are you in possession of your mind, two arms, two legs
Hands and feet work good why stand here and beg
If you handicapped or elderly sure I'll come out the pocket
But I won't contribute to the poisoning of drug addicts and
    alcoholics
I've seen these same guys out at the crack of dawn
Doing whatever they have to get the hit on
That used to be called job hunting

Critical Condition (Part 2)

I can understand if his point of views and demeanor may be off putting.
But think about it like this: he lives in another world. Get over it.

The white man this and the white man that
They hold us down no opportunity for blacks
Lies and propaganda fed to us by officials
That propagate the conditions we live in
When truth is every day people get along in this place
Regardless of what color our skins is
You don't hear about racism until you turn on the news
They act like everybody is a Nazi if you don't share their views
If that's true and I'm running with Hitler who's playing the Jews
I'm not saying racism and all that stuff ain't real
If it's a wound on the nation quit pulling off the scab
Maybe it will heal

Critical Condition (Part 3)

Whether you think so or not, he is a man of integrity, and he loves his family. Just like everyone else, he is looking in the window of the lives of his neighbor, passing his life and existence off on them. If I can do, you can too, but can they really?

The condition we live in is critical
It's so many who refuse to try even a little
Life is a gift so precious it's squandered living reckless
You need a pencil and paper maybe so here's a checklist

1) Physical life is nice, but did you know we can all live twice? That's right, the second comes bundled with Christ.
2) The actions that we do and the decisions that we make determine future results of situations those same actions create.
3) No matter what you may think or what you been told it's only one way possible to save the soul.
4) Death is found at birth experienced at the end of our stay on Earth and witnessed by all at the judgment.
5) I can't get anyone to listen or pay attention. All I can do is keep myself out of critical condition

Let My People Go! (Part 1)

In this counterparts, universe, organized religion has been outlawed. Well, that may be too strong of a term. It's been highly regulated and co-opted by unscrupulous government officials seeking ways to control and mislead the populace. Which by the way was against the constitution of his America. He organized a weekend worth of marches in DC. This is Saturday's speech outside the capitol.

The Bible says that Moses stood before Pharaoh asking for the
freedom to enjoy the grace and love of the Lord
(the crowd yelled) Let my people go!
Physically they were enslaved to build monuments to imaginary
gods and cities they couldn't even live in
(the crowd yelled) Let my people go!
The Lord raised up a champion to lead his people free
Holy wars were waged and after eleven decisive victories
Ten plagues and a mass drowning he had no other choice but to
(the crowd yelled) Let my people go!
This country was built on the same foundation as ancient Egypt
we of African descent can look back hundreds of years
Find our fathers murdered our mothers raped as we built mon-
uments to our oppressors and cities we couldn't even live
in
(the crowd yelled) Let my people go!
Centuries have passed nineteen, twenty, now twenty-one we
still enslaved this time to luxury
But I think we could and should look deeper than that
Because often our truths are covered up by carefully crafted facts
(the crowd yelled) Let my people go!

Let My People Go! (Part 2)

Remember in this America that all truth is sponsored and delivered to the people by the government. After all, somebody has to protect them from misinformation and disinformation When the government corners the market and monopolizes the truth, the people suffer.

On this Sunday at the end of his speech, the counter protestors showed up, paid operatives dressed in black tactical gear and armed with melee weapons. They stormed into the peaceful marchers creating havoc and killing key leadership, including the organizer. Talk about famous last words.

Our forefathers would work together fleeing to the north but
    nowadays the shackles of iniquity lead us to believe that
    we're free and nothing's wrong
These chains are placed around our necks at the moment we
    know earthly life
Everyone has worn them at one time or another one chain dif-
    ferent links
Murder theft pride and hate just to name a few
        (the crowd yelled) Let my people go!
The Lord has once again raised up a champion to lead his peo-
    ple free
The Template Man the first and only of his kind
The power of eternity clothed in the skin of mortality
After one decisive victory over the grave to put it to you blunt
This dude changed the game
        (the crowd yelled) Let my people go!
The sacrifice made by one man freed generations yet to come
But still we fumble around in darkness when there is a beacon
    of light

That beams right in your face
          (the crowd yelled) Let my people go!
We are a stubborn lot with self-destructive tendencies
Greed courses through our veins we are now puppets
To an evil so absolute that many times my heart breaks at the
          thought
That at least two thirds of the people I meet
On the streets are the walking dead
Free yourself no one is holding you but you
That price was paid thousands of years ago when the grave was
          defeated
And the Lord demanded the power of death to
          (the crowd yelled) Let my people go!

A Few Good Men (Part 1)

This counterpart's America is another place on a tipping point. This man lives in a world where feminists have frankly gone too far. The attacks on traditional masculinity are brutal and socially accepted. It's as if a man now needs permission to be. His response was to reopen the local boys club, which had been closed for years. The grand opening weekend is captured here.

A woman once told me there were no good men to be found
But every time she had a guy all she did was criticize and put
    him down
Dog him out like a hound that just escaped from the pound
See this miss was missing what's needed to be a missus to a
    mister
Some think the answer is just sex that is sure road to
To being alone, bitter-hearted and perplexed
Because the dude she gave it to move on to the next
She really wanted to earn his respect well keep your legs closed
    for a minute
Put both yourselves to the test
Talk to him learn about him men carry unexplained pain
We been conditioned to grin and bear it not cry or complain
The way to man's heart bypasses his stomach start with his brain

A Few Good Men (Part 2)

With the crowd's general excitement and local support for his venture, it's surprising it wasn't successful. The crowd for his Saturday grand opening was huge. Personally, I think it was outside interference. Somebody in his country did not want strong capable men. I wonder why?

Now this is for my men each one of you to me is more than a
    friend
It's like we all brothers even of other colors are still my next of
    kin
It's time to answer the call and rise like the sun
Give up these guns and impact the lives of our sons
We got to first overcome our pasts
Stop letting the things that happened back then still last
No excuse take our responsibilities with dignity and class
When you treat your kids like strangers constantly expose them
    to danger
Skeletons in the closet looking like coat hangers
You get a warped perception of manhood
Corner tough guys or mama boys can't even stand good
Scared to live on his own like a man should
Instead he sleeps in the same kid bed at home with his mom
Screaming that he grown while hiding from his problems
It takes more than age to make you a man
Like it takes more than a thumb to make up a hand

A Few Good Men (Part 3)

This Sunday crowd made national news. That was when he got on the radar of the wrong people. This was sad because I think he would have a real difference if he wasn't murdered. It's been said he was killed by a woman; it was never solved like most murders involving Black men. I get the impression sometimes that murder is okay as long as it's a Black man.

Evil triumphs when good men do nothing
God made men so without him we just bluffing
A man's perception of himself how he looks at being he
That's the first thing *God* wants to change is how your third eye
    sees
Let's try to see man from our creators point of you
You'll see it's not a lot of good men only a few
We should be leaders and warriors both brave and true
With a code of conduct now ask yourself is that you
If it ain't then let the supreme artist paint another picture
That will fit you like a masterpiece
Then you will be a piece of the master
A man the way it was intended to be

Fish Flopping (Part 1)

I want to be clear about these entries. At the times I received these, he was a recovering addict and alcoholic. All the experience I have with controlled substances of this guy's level is only what I have witnessed in the lives of others. I support his desire to be clean, I won't judge. Just pass on the information. This was the night he had enough and could go on no more living like this.

I'll take it from the top I would always say I could stop
If that's true why am I on the floor again like a fish that flops
I started as kid with cigarettes there it is your gateway drug
In my youth I lived black and wild and cigarettes got to pricey
I moved to black and milds and all this time I had been drink-
    ing for years
Cheap stuff mad dog night train and Colt 45 beer
I drank this by the case the label read malt liquor
All I found it was quicker to make me sicker
My brains is addled rattled from years of abuse
I don't think its repairable no matter what I do
If this is a fight I been losing too long
My ex told me I been fighting this all wrong
She introduced me to *God* and how he is eternally strong
Packed her bags then she was gone

Fish Flopping (Part 2)

The first part represents the night of determination and clarity. This part is a year later when he is at a local park telling his story to kids at the basketball court. He has struggled with but managed to maintain his sobriety. I wish I could have had more time with him instead of some of the others that submitted entries over the years.

I had a secret desire to die from an overdose
Or cirrhosis of the liver pills, heroin, cocaine, and fentanyl
It didn't matter to me I would try it all
In the spirit world a dungeon door swung ajar
Upon leaving the cell that I dwelled
I seen *God's* glory twinkling like a star
I was shown my life to be hollow fulfillment awaited me
But only if I followed hills valleys and sharp turns
The road gets twisted I keep my head on a swivel now
Life moves so fast I don't want to miss it or dive off a cliff
It's not fun or exciting so many friends made over the years
They don't stop dying
There are people I know that didn't smoke or drink
Became addicts after visiting a shrink
They tell us it's a war on drugs. Wrong!
Our government is so in love with it
They've been feeding it to us all along
It ain't the street drug sold by elite thugs
Want my life back from all the years
Of traveling needle tracks no more fish flopping

The Weekend the Weak Ends (Part 1)

Now this one is strange. This man is in a psych ward. He received a vision from God while driving to work. He crashed into a school bus. People were hurt, but no one died. What makes this scenario even stranger is that all he can remember is the vision; he has total amnesia except for what God showed him. This is Friday intake.

I drop to my knees hold my hands to the sky
When I envisioned Jesus Christ the son of *God* being crucified
Pierced through his side crown of thorns on my Lord's head
Nails driven through his hands and feet
An inscription is written in Latin, Hebrew, and Greek
This is the king of the Jews beside him two men speak
One said if you the Christ save us then yourself
The other spoke of paradise he knew no time was left

The Weekend the Weak Ends (Part 2)

Understand this: everything he said that weekend I have listed here. I know it's hard to believe. I know what I saw and heard, whether you believe me or not, that's up to you. I just have to get this out of my head. It's your problem now. Have fun.

Nailed to the cross an innocent man life lost
To mend our relationship with *God* that was the cost
When he died the curtain in the temple tore in two
That represents a barrier put by a sin we did not do
This is all true not a story that's simply told
This is real truth search for yourself and you'll be showed
The lamb told them before in three days he'd be raised
So they guarded his resting place with armed soldiers just in
    case
The stone that sealed the master's tomb was heavy, cold, and
    gray
On the third day an angel came and rolled that stone away
Daily crucify our flesh life is nothing but tests
Full of distress and temptations and that's at its best
John 3:16 I have nothing else to say
I know what I saw us seeking the father through the son
And the Holy Spirit led the way

The Three Rs (Part 1)

This guy here is an actual minister. Started out as a teen. Faith healing lying on hands. The whole nine yards. He ended up cheating on his wife, got busted, the IRS came down on him, and somehow he went to prison. He never lost his faith actually being in jail made his relationship with his creator even stronger. When he got out, he spoke at his old church.

Repentance
I felt like we're separated by an invisible barrier
I was sickly and weak patient zero the plague carrier
My grip, my sanity, my humanity steady slipping
I keep being haunted by reenactments of bad decisions
My heart bleeds an apology that fights for the chance of a sec-
    ond time
I feel like I'm back in my right mind no more distractions to
    take your place
And my wife stayed true and faithful even though I'm disgraced
I'm wearing sackcloth throwing ashes on my head and face

The Three *R*s (Part 2)

He was invited back a second week, more people showed up, and they even prepared a secret fund to help him and his wife financially. It wasn't a lot, but God can turn eight dollars into eight million.
If that's in line with his will for you.

Restoration
I've been placed back to my station X has returned but I still
    can't solve the equation
The missing link the stopper that goes in the sink
The train on the track of the thoughts that I think the ice in
    the rink
The one who programmed my eyes to involuntarily blink
Regrets are chains that hold us in place like a sticky paste
I'm looking to be restored like spring leaves
God I beseech thee not to ignore me
Repentance is the first R. Now please restore me

The Three Rs (Part 3)

I'm sure by now you have noticed a pattern in many of the lives of my counterparts. After another invitation to speak, the largest crowd in church history was there, along with the media to cover his story of redemption. News cameras only made things worse. As at the end of his message, two mass shooters, one on either side of the church, began to open fire.

Redirection
So when I'm faced with the final inspection
Well done good and faithful servant my greeting at reception
My perceptions mean nothing when everything I ever seen is
    all lies
Most of your blessings and lessons can't be seen with mortal eyes
So if you decide it's time to end my ride
Please recognize that I continued to strive
For repentance restoration and redirection before I died

The City Limits (Part 1)

This counterpart was a politician. His first foray into public service was against an incumbent senator who had been in office since before Black people could vote. Living in a small town, in a small state, no one had run against this man in over twenty years. This entry is the one that got him taken seriously.

Darkness at noon real soon our sun will be consumed
In a midafternoon tomb perpetual night but only for our lost
    nation
Who's been incarcerated, hated, and feared while treading on
    snakes
He has dominion that means we rule we hire dumb teachers
To teach smart kids in school
The solutions given to them sound like they came from cartoons
I'm blaming you Mr. Career Man Mr. Public Servant
Washington, DC, limits hopes and dreams none of us are
    important
I know about things they did that never got reported
Abortion is the leading cause of death among blacks
And if you think you have that right then keep thinking that
They teach mythology in school
But if you sit alone praying quietly can't have that
We are all the faces of lost history and mind erasing
Cops beat blacks till they drop and say he fell when chasing
Politicians like you make promises they have no plans to keep
Collecting campaign contributions from the most corrupt
    creeps

The City Limits (Part 2)

Before he threw his hat in this race, he and his best friend had established themselves by producing and starring in an adult-themed cartoon. It swept the world by storm. He dropped out of the senate race at the behest of his family. Death threats sent to his family; his wife got fired from her job for no apparent good reason; his kids were being bullied online and in school. It was decided that he had more to lose than an election. This was his last political speech before he left the race.

Within the limits of the city it's a gamble for our souls
Seven and eleven drop from heaven snake eyes every other roll
Three to four will get you gold five to six losing all self-control
Eight to nine is cash from something stole or dope sold
Ten will get you dames with no name in a hotel
Two and twelve that says go directly to jail
Do not pass go bypass that on your way to hell
I'd rather see you impeached, kicked out, or put in jail
This fact has been laid out loving *God* seemed to have played out
Our minds have been cast way out
Those in power seem to want us to stay out
What is the worth of a humans life me, myself, I have no price
But I do have the inner peace and insight that came with Christ
Social scavengers vultures of our own culture
In *God* we trust no more we worship sculptures
It's easy to say that was b.c this is a.d
But we praise money power and shapes of attractive ladies
To a politician like you the city is a collection of buildings
To bring in revenue but what about the citizens especially our
    children
America was once called the shining city on a hill
But what they didn't say is that crap pours downhill

Save the Kids (Part 1)

This counterpart is the family man. His wife and three daughters are what has shaped and defined his adult life. His world suffered under a man-made pandemic. Several evil rogue governments sought a change in the global order. They released highly virulent contagion around the world. After closing churches, small businesses, and schools, he began to see negative changes in his girls. He and his wife started going to school board meetings. First visit.

I can sit on my porch and see young men with flames ablaze
    passing the weed torch
Young women with no modesty I had to ask my wife baby is
    them panties or shorts
You closed the schools while social media made it cool for kids
    to break the rules
Making fun and beating up other kids who ain't got the latest
    pair of tennis shoes
It's a shame they can tell you every weapon on video games
But fail basic math tests and don't know state capital names
Good old Mr. White ain't never really did black folks right
That's why in the ghettos schools been gettin' closed day and
    night
But he can build casinos and stadiums at every stop light
I didn't graduate high school for years that filled me with regret
That time of life can snuff a child's light out like a cigarette
But now it's closed down tore down by who Mr. Mayor
Whose only concern is big business and bank rolls of ball players
Its kids in penitentiaries with a lifetime bid
Because the evil they saw is the evil they did
When I was young it was all about the Benjamins
And you can make crack like this

I had to ask myself did I want my girls hearing crap like this
I said no send them to a good school work hard for them
To have advantages that skipped by you…isn't that what every
    parent here wants to do?

To hell with saving whales let's keep our kids out of jail
They're the future versions of our past selves

Save the Kids (Part 2)

Have you noticed a pattern with the returners? This second appearance brought news cameras, then all of a sudden, a small town in a small state became the epicenter of what would change the political landscape for years to come; this was his second meeting.

When I was young I cut school I thought it was fun
Even skipped town once scared I broke the law and I was on
    the run
Please kids listen to me when I say this to you
I know what it's like to feel alone with no one to turn to
But there is someone always in your corner believe it or not
He's a bodyguard best friend and he loves you a lot
Many times I should have been dead in these streets
The same one that wants to rescue you is the one that rescued
    me
Yesterday I bought a newspaper because the front page
Read kids killing kids in the school the same age
Dude where they get the guns from? What happened to their
    minds?
Questions I never ask. Kids killing kids. Why not
They see grown folks do it all the time someone listen to me
Anybody please parents put aside your differences
Show them what they need to see
Men stop beating your women woman start respecting your
    man
When a child is born it's a literal clean slate waiting to be
    programmed

To hell with savings whales let's keep our kids out of jail
They're the future versions of our past selves

Save the Kids (Part 3)

Now does this guy sound like a domestic terrorist? To the feds and their plans to turn kids into drug-addled hypersexual narcissistic crybaby bullies, anyone who would oppose that is a domestic terrorist. He disappeared the next day and was never seen again.

I ain't no one special I just like to be honest and real
Morally the world is wounded that's our job to heal
The youth teach the truth instead their mentalities we pollute
Poisoning our children is the only thing the unions seem to do
In order to save these kids we need to watch who raised these
    kids
Because our evil government is looking to take away our kids
Some of you treat your kids so darn mean
I don't know why you surprised when they rebel and scheme
We told 'em don't talk to strangers to protect them from dangers
But now it's the classroom curriculum which is getting stranger
There's your danger by the way Christmas was never about
    Santa
It was always about a child in a manger

To hell with saving whales let's keep our kids out of jail
They're the future versions of our past selves

The Mystery of History (Part 1)

This counterpart was ahead of the curve in terms of government intrusion of public education. He is a stay-at-home dad and homeschools his five kids. The curriculum was such that his neighbors enrolled their kids. This is the lesson that hooked his neighbors.

Chapter 1: The Creation

Big bang evolution all that's an illusion
Confusions created by men to control outcomes and conclusions
We are on the road to ruin for the evil we've been doing
World history is no mystery if it's the truth your pursuing
See I heard life started out of a random explosion
A destructive blast of force?
That always sounded to me like the wrong idea was chosen
What exploded and how did that create anything
Grass? Water? Love? Life? Human beings?
We deny ourselves an expanded insight
By thinking that going to college is somehow going to improve
    your life
You learn what the instructor was taught
And he is eager to sell you the same lies that he bought
Everything that has been created was created by a creator
Even conceptual realties like the one called the equator
It's written in my favorite book that all creation took six days
But how long is a day to someone that existed always?

The Mystery of History (Part 2)

He was soon reported by envious people with different point of views. Instead of respecting his rights, it was said he violated them by not including their kids even though they never wanted their kids in his classes. People are small and petty sometimes. His impromptu school got shut; his kids forced back into public schools. This was his last lesson.

Chapter 2: The History of Man

Adam and Eve the garden they had to leave
Cain killed Abel basically over jealousy
In turn Cain received a mark on his face
Adam fathered Seth which was Abel replaced
Seth had Enosh who in turn fathered Kenan
Mahalalel is his son and his son is Jared
Whose son Enoch lived 365 years then disappeared
His son was Methuseleh who had Lamech who had Noah
Three sons Shem, Japheth, and Ham
Shem being the older
Then the rains came forty days and forty nights
It rained until the highest peaks were out of sight
Eventually the Earth began to dry
From there *He* gave all humanity a second try
Our human ancestral lineage vast and immense
For homework read the book of Genesis

Class dismissed

WWJD (Part 1)

This counterpart is a grandfather. His only daughter was murdered during a domestic violence incident involving her now incarcerated ex-husband. He is currently raising her two children. On his Earth in his America, the country is in the middle of nationwide riots over the perceived racism of law enforcements. His grandkids got arrested at one such event. The next three days, he spent trying to better understand how to reach them before he lost them.

Would he sell dope be fond of cigarette smoke
Or school us on life with biblical quotes
Would he pursue riches call our women hoes and bitches
Or would he show us all love even those not religious
Would he steal, would he rape, would he hesitate
At lending a helping hand to get us through heaven's gates
Would he get twelve more disciples of different races and colors
All under one father so all twelve is brothers
Would he get inebriated off booze rob you for your shoes
Kill and enslave others who hair not blond and eyes not blue
Would he sell his body to the highest bidder
Or just do nothing with his life 'cause he lazy and a quitter
Would he crack jokes breath in crack smoke
Or would he just bring it to the ghettos just to give it to black
    folks
Would he turn the other cheek and leave revenge to *God*
Or get mad and come back with a firing squad
Would he wear a white hood or a red rag
Make weapons of war designed to make us extinct like black
    flag
Would he cry for the condition his *Father's* world is in
And do what he did last time and die for our sins

WWJD (Part 2)

The world had changed so much since he raised a child. The girls just sighed and rolled their eyes at him. Told him he was too old to understand what was happening in the world. He just shook his head and tried again the next morning at breakfast.

Would he care for us like a shepherd do his flock
Would he be evil like us and kill one another with glocks
Some of us worship the *Lord* one day Sunday
Then back doing the same dirt Monday
I don't think he condones part-time Christians
But that's like a bad word now I've learned to listen
To what they don't mention would he deny us
Like some deny he exists
Nope, he keeps his arms open with your name on the list
Would he start wars with other countries over oil and money?
Would he laugh at famine stricken nations who people go
    hungry
Would he help the homeless the sick and distressed
We all know that answer a resounding yes
Would he cry for the condition his *Father's* world is in
And do what he did last time and die for our sins

WWJD (Part 3)

So he takes the girls to church on Sunday morning. After a rousing service, on the way home, the girls seemed much more receptive to the day three discussion.

Would he practice what he preaches or talk to hear himself talk
Would you let him hold your hand on life's long walk
The name alone messiah should inspire
His blood is a shield that lets you walk through life's fires
It don't expire and He didn't retire
He's the son of the living *God* your reservation to heaven buyer
What would Jesus do
What pleases the one that sent him or what pleases you
To tell you girls the truth I am an old man now
And I'll be glad when he returns so I can watch the righteous
    rise
And witness the wicked left to burn

Strawberry Rose (Part 1)

Another female counterpart. She became a drug addict in junior high. It started as a means of coping with abuse she received at home from her older brothers. It's hard for me to write these types of entries. I wanted this tour to be a source of strength and inspiration, but the lives of certain counterparts are so sad; it's sometimes hard for me to swallow. This is one such story.

He is kingpin status when up to his benz
Came the same woman he saw chilling with his friends
She looked beyond amazing as she sauntered his direction
She says hi I'm Rose he gets an instant erection
She gets in the ride he puts the pedal to the floor
As he drives he wants her body more and more
He pulls up at the crib starts unbuttoning her shirt
She takes his other hand places in between her skirt
He thinks he about get it he really want to hit it
She pushes him back hold up wait a minute
I know what you want but you got something for me
Cash or product but no one rides for free
They go in the house he toss boulders over his shoulders
Thirty seconds later this dude all over her
He wakes the next morning with plans to hit again
When he looks for her she gone along with his wallet and benz

Strawberry Rose (Part 2)

Part 1 took place on Friday. And please don't think I am anti-woman in any way. I have to deliver it the way I received it. Remember I don't need or want anyone's approval. I just want to help and be helped and maybe this will help someone. It helps me to deliver it.

It's a Saturday night inside of a club
She walks in white looking like a dove from above
She climbs on top of the bar shaking her breasts
Grinding her hips these dudes standing around lickin' the lips
Even the men in there with chicks get yelled at and ushered out
    quick
She speaks to the remaining men in the place
What I'm doing up here is an example a taste
I'm breaking all off up in here if you like tonight
But I gotta see all the cash and dope in plain sight
She made ten grand in cash another ten for her blasts
Sixteen dudes and one chick made a day and a half past

Strawberry Rose (Part 3)

I had more visits with her at the time of writing this than any other 4 in total. I often wish I could physically interact with my counterparts. I would try and save some of them from the fates I know that awaits. But that's not how this works. I only get to see and hear sometimes it's unbearably painful other times unbearably beautiful. You can decide what or if they mean Anything to you.

She ain't no hooker you won't find her on street corners
But you will find a long line of men that want her
Ballers, hard workers, even lames are treated the same
If you ain't got what she wants you don't get past her name
She'll smoke weed, do rocks, poke needles through her socks
Pop pills to get a thrill she'll drink bleach over the rocks
She is rotten in her core beautiful outside
The first time she hit the pipe it was like picking up a knife
Cutting your wrists and hope that she don't bleed
At one point it was fun now it's a life-consuming need
Wherever she goes she gets lustful stares and glances
From the young and the old even those in romances
Anyone stepping to her making advances you taking serious
    chances

Strawberry Rose (Part 4)

I can't tell you why four entries were received from Rose. I do know it was important. So I do the job. I really hope there is a benefit to someone out there from this tragic life.

It's a Monday morning she walks down the avenue
White leather jacket skintight dress that's blue
She got that strut with that switch she Kardashian thick
Dressed was spray-painted on couldn't find nary a stitch
Black land cruiser pulls up to the curb
He opens the door she gets in without a word
An older white guy a well-to-do lawyer
He tells her he been after her since he saw her
Two weeks ago across from the mall at hojo's
She says currently if you got currency we can rock and roll
If you don't then stop the truck now I gotta go
He takes her to an unfamiliar section of town
He snatches Rose out the car throws the girl to the ground
He drags her inside pushes her down to the floor
She breaks free but he grabs her by the weave
Pushes her on the couch yelling you don't leave
Until I'm done you know you like it you came here for the fun
He bends her over the couch rip up her dress
She struggling hard she doesn't want to be here anymore
I can feel her distress
He reaches behind the couch pulls something from under the
    seat
He considers her subhuman a rabid dog in heat
It's too bad that Rose didn't see the nine
Because he came and she went at the same time

Daddy's Home (Part 1)

Before we begin, understand that this man is pure evil. Out of all the things I have had to witness over the years from my counterparts, this guy is the worst. Thankfully, I only had to endure two entries.

She heard the key in the door telling her that he's here
She quickly covered with sweat her heart and mind knew fear
She ran up to her room and realized she didn't clean it
And if he found out she'd be in for more than a beating
She felt like cotton was shoved in her mouth
And a fist squeezed her heart
Just the moonlight through her window illuminated the dark
Heard a voice downstairs couldn't tell who it is
Because the door was closed and her hands covered her ears
Footsteps coming up the stairs
She told her mom once what daddy was doing it's like she didn't
　　　care
Her mom called her a lying whore smacked her so hard she fell
　　　down to the floor
At first it was nice when he rocked her to sleep
When he would lie in bed with her about three nights a week
That's when she was nine now she sixteen
For seven long years she's been daddy's midnight plaything
She's been pregnant three times he forced her to get abortions
He lied to her mother placed the blame on secret boyfriends
But she's never had one daddy won't let her
He said she was his and no other man would get her
The room door opens slow and it's him standing there
She had to look twice she thought she saw horns in his hair
He got in bed with her and his touch was cold as stone
He whispered in her ear daddy's home

Daddy's Home (Part 2)

See what I mean? Look, let's just get through this one together. However, watch "karma, justice, reciprocity, and God's vengeance," whatever you want to call it.

It's on display here. Pay attention.

Daddy told her he loves her that's why he does it
At first she believed him now she knows he doesn't
Because before her he did the same thing to her cousin
She can't look him in the eyes she is so filled with shame
She used to think it was her fault she didn't know who else to
    blame
Is it hers for letting him, her mother's for neglecting him
Or is it daddy's for making her to scared to tell on him
Once she got away screaming and running
He just told her mother he was whipping her for something
He's turned daddy's little girl into daddy's other woman
What can she do what can she say
No one believes her and once again daddy's on his way
When no one was home she called her cousin on the phone
She came over so she wouldn't be scared and alone
They decided together they had a better chance
To convince anyone he had been manhandling both of their
    pants
They went down together to the police
He got picked up at work and is yet to be released
She doesn't fear the cold of his touch or that evil in his tone
When he would whisper in ear daddy's home
           Because daddy's gone

The Ring (Part 1)

This man fell in love at first sight. Something I personally scoff at. But this is his quest not just for love and acceptance but the truth in it. This one makes me a little jealous.

Chance meeting casual greeting pain tattooed to my heart
My life is bleeding, sick, and tired of the past that's why I'm
    leaving
We both have a seat on the ground my head's down
When I look up all she sees is my face locked in a frown
She says you look like a king that just lost his crown
We talk for a minute more then the bus rolls up
She sits in the middle in the back is where I hold up
Truth is I ain't never had much game
That's why I sat down without getting her name
My never builds halfway through the ride
After talking more I find her beauty extends inside
I missed my stop it's all good because it's summer
I walked all the way home totally forgot to get her number
Time passes slower than frozen molasses
All I know is her name she light skinned and where glasses
She touched my very heart from the start
To me her beauty exceeds any man made work of art
I even left work early to sit at the bus stop late
During that month I was on the hunt I got my act straight
It was a Friday morning the twentieth of June
Got on the bus eye contact I could feel her heart swoon
I sit next to her we start smiling and talking
Got off at the same stop exchanged numbers while we walking
For the first time ever I could hear angels sing
I praise the *Lord* for her that's why I got her this ring

The Ring (Part 2)

I'm a closet romantic, so this guy here really inspired me to search for what he has.

It's obvious he is in love with her. But does she feel the same? Do you know how many men have loved a woman who didn't love them in return? That's a dangerous place to be with certain types of people. I wonder.

Knock on wood so far so good
I'm surprised when I found out we live in the same hood
Five minutes going five minutes coming back
And if it's 911 I'm there in thirty seconds flat
For me it was love at first sight and to my personal delight
We made love in a tree house under a starry night
We burned incense on the porch touch on our histories
Meditation techniques purge us of past miseries
You been through so much in your life but you still stay strong
Men beat you and mistreat you but that stops when I came
    along
This is destiny *God's* divine plan
That we be together from earth to the promised land
We can be a force for good something constructive
We can be a force for evil something disruptive
That choice is ours but since our insides ain't sour
We are going to love life with all the power
Of a couple who has discovered the endless energy
Generated by our remaining hours
I thought we shared the same values, hopes, and dreams
That's why I bought her this ring

The Ring (Part 3: The Vow)

I really didn't think he would get a happy ending since so few of my counterparts have. But she said yes, and this was his vow at his wedding.

Before I met you I loved you your hair
Your smile your penetrating stare
It's as if all my life was a triangle
When it should have been a square
No bounds at all no fear to fall my trust in you is true
This day you become all I ever hoped
My best friend my reality anchor my mental lifeboat
Some said we weren't meant to be
But they don't know what we don't show
What *God* has done with us makes us eternally strong
I was humbled when you became my fiancée
I'm honored that you decided to be my wife
Queen for a day but that day will last the rest of your life
I love you my missing rib has been reconnected to my side

Blood Transfusions (Part 1)

I'm looking for life relief from strife forsake the darkness
    embrace the light
It's glowing bright chasing away the demons that stalk my night
I stand under a waterfall of blood it's a rushing flash flood
Of nothing but kindness and love straight from above came the
    prince of peace
With the spirit descending like a dove I wear it like a body glove
Let the blood drip from my lips to my toe tips
Without *God* I was like a Cadillac on a racetrack
With a tire full of tacks with a drunk driver behind the wheel
    addicted to crack
How do I face that I don't want to taste that
Blood clots, blood stains. Blood transfuses, blood bathes
But only the blood of the lamb can purify. Under the red cross
    blood saves

Blood Transfusions (Part 2)

He is a divorced father who hasn't seen his kids in a longtime. The family courts can sometimes be cruel and unfair to fathers. If you haven't seen it firsthand, trust me you don't know. When a man pays support to the kids and still isn't allowed to see them over some nonsense, he in essence is paying another man a salary to raise his kids, at least that's my opinion.

I should have had a vasectomy somewhere around twenty-three
Probably never should have gotten married either
I think that was the beginning of the end for me
Its life in the blood that's what the Bible said
Blood sacrifice is when something else dies in your stead
I want to know what's wrong in their heads is it the brain fled
Or is it somewhere starving to death malnourished and underfed
I feed mine cups of living water and loaves of life bread
I'm letting go over my past now I'm focused on a future ever last
I walked both sides of the fence and believe me
Over here is much greener grass

The Inner City Lullaby (Part 1)

This counterpart has only been alive three days. I saw his life flash before my eyes. This is what I saw.

Go to sleep little baby don't let it drive you crazy
Life for you ain't a bowl of cherries neither is it gravy
It's going to be hard look where you growing up
You may not eat if your mom monthly check ain't showing up
She is fourteen your dad is twenty-nine
She thought she was grown and he was after young behind
Socially resisted publicly assisted themes the projects
One-bedroom dump with rats as your pets
You grow up alone becoming one with the streets
By the time you nine you hustling dope to fiends
When you turn ten you get your first gat
Once you take that step boy ain't no turning back
As I watch you sleeping I'm standing here shaking my head
It's got to be a way out something else for you instead
Born a statistic in the land of the free and the home of the slaves
The *Lord's* strength has no length so little baby be brave
Maybe you can be a different case
I'm disturbed as I watch you sleeping with tears pouring down
  your face
It's a lot of kids like you some will live and some will die
Go to sleep little baby to the inner city lullaby

The Inner City Lullaby (Part 2)

It's such a familiar story with my counterparts. I want to help them, but I can't. I can only write his life away like I did mine.

Dream little baby of peace and tranquility
When your eleven you'll be in correctional facility
Juvenile detention for possession of a double deuce
Sticking up some dude for his Jordans and his loot
Fourteen locked away three times
Striving to be a shot caller a baller the heroes in your eyes
Smoking weed selling dope every girl has the same name
Going to jail don't scare you man that's just part of the game
Whatever your crew do you do if you don't you ain't true to
Your homies your phony they act as if they never knew you
Influenced to be a truant a soldier with no limits
Don't be hypnotized by the lies that's nothing but a gimmick
It's called entertainment you will know it has mental enslavement
You got the heart of a lion but the brains of wet pavement
Getting paid by any means hook, crook, or scandalous schemes
Your plan is to get all you can ain't that the American dream?
Black males are born with two strikes we give ourselves the third
Stop playing with stereotypes of self-entitlement and demanding
For what you think you deserve
You still young but it's like each passing day you being hung
We were raised in different places but I'm straight where you
    from
It's a lot of kids like you some will live and some will die
Go to sleep little baby to the inner city lullaby

The Inner City Lullaby (Part 3)

It's said everybody loves babies. But not everyone needs to have them. I lost my kids early in their lives and wasn't allowed to see them. So parenthood is a joy I never fully experienced, and then again everything is not for everybody.

Beware the nightmares little baby they stalk your sleep
Now you supplying your mothers habit a couple times a week
When you stop with the blow she shows you the door
So you move in with one of your girlfriends
As you have no other place to go
You seventeen making moves with your friends
Your girl wants you to stop scared of cop-sponsored end
You tell her no you a man now you grown
After all you livin' on your own sharing a home with a two-
     month-old newborn
You got no job talking and acting like you part of the mob
But your fellas is jealous you the next one they rob
They don't wear masks they want you to know who it was
All cash and drugs and gunfire was not an outlier
They filled him with slugs
It's a lot of kids like you some will live and some will die
Rest in peace little baby to the inner city lullaby

The Doomsday Prophet (Part 1)

This one here I could have included in the stand-alones. Why didn't I?
The multiple entries along with. Well, his story explains itself.

His mother was a drug addict instead of blood in her veins
There was a cocktail of everything from heroin to cocaine
So many holes in her soul, heart, and brain
She had her only son during a thunderous downpouring rain
She was high stratosphere feeling no pain
And he was born already trapped in now hereditary chains
The stress of it all shut her body down yeah she died
From his throne on high
The Lord heard the newborn's cry
He sent mercy in the form of two passersby
A minister at a local church and this pastor's wife
This reverend had been raised in them streets
A thug type most of his life thought he would never preach
His wife, his partner, his right hand he calls her baby girl
And sadly her womb was barren like the landscape
Of a desolate world
They discovered the mom and child truly a horrible sight
A young woman dead with a baby between her legs
Under the streetlight the baby's cries echo into the night
They made plans to adopt at first light
Named him Samson and never kept it secret about his birthnight
Growing up his parents was his best friends taught him to hate
    sin
And the condition of the planet not the people therein
Beware the three things that destroy most men
Money, power, and the pursuit of the wrong women

Respect discipline and determination
Will save you from most situations but the number one of all
Jesus and his gift of salvation

The Doomsday Prophet (Part 2)

This is why I debated on where to place his entries. You should be able to see it by now. This guy is a stand-alone, but I have gotten so much material over the years.

Anyway many days have past at long last
He was nineteen when he threw everything he owned in the
    trash
Or sold it for cash told his parents *God* said his time had come
And for them not to be sad
Two hundred dollars and some food in a sack
In his hands held a staff he carved from a tree
A project he himself started at thirteen
The most important item he had for his survival
Was given to him the day after they found him his Bible
From then on everywhere he went he walked
Whenever he had the chance he would sit with strangers and
    talk
Every Sunday he visits a different church
And after service chat up the pastors about the work
He sometimes would get fed and a place to stay
After a couple of days the Doomsday Prophet was on his way
He would only except what was offered never ask for any pay

The Doomsday Prophet (Part 3)

I tell you this is one of my favorites. Please don't assume my goal is to shove religion at you. It's not. I don't care what you believe. Allow the essence of the entry to soak in. I don't want or need for any of you to change to fit me. Because I don't plan on doing that for you. Let the essence of the entries to soak in.

Eventually he got notoriety and was seen on TV
People were intrigued by the likes of a man previously unseen
They offered him money for an exclusive interview
He told them keep their payment dinner would do
The press made arrangements at a five-star place
He turned that down with a look of disgust on his face
He said follow me and led them to a soup kitchen
And told the reporter the camera needs their attention
He says but this day I tell you there is help for these people
These things we see here are temporary at best
The flesh is born dead eternal is the soul that's left
I have given away everything I possess
To be clothed in *God's* righteousness and nothing else
He looked staring in the camera sincerity and truth living in
    his eyes
Please search for the salvation granted from on high
In other words serve the *Lord* or die

Dearly Departed

Watch your step as you exit the ride
Double-check to make sure you left nothing inside
No kids, wallets, or bags all that will get tossed in the trash
Our journey together this time has ended
But I get the feeling I just added to my friend's list
This ride is available to you now, whenever, and however
You may find it useful when overwhelmed by fear and terror
A dry place if you will from life's bad weather
As we speak right now I'm preparing a chapter 2
It'll be coming soon to a universe near you so stay tuned
Thanks again for helping me humanity
From every Samson Brown everywhere we love you!

About the Author

Samson Brown was born an African American[*] male in Brooklyn, New York, in the early seventies. He was raised, shaped, and taught the values that come from an abused childhood. As an adult, he was diagnosed with *paranoid schizophrenia with psychotic tendencies*. That's the clinical name anyway. He doesn't call it that to himself, it's just the way he thinks. If he allows a bunch of overly educated, know-it-all narcissists define his brain as handicapped, then that means his thoughts are broken and only they know what's best for him. For example, pills and other drugs; strangers who can only see you as a patient, not a person; and dependence on an overly taxed system of social safety nets.

He's cool. It took a long time to come to this way of thinking. One thing he hope leaps off this tour for you is the roles faith and love played and can play in the lives of humans if you let them. He's not trying to force a narrative or a belief system on anyone on this journey. In order to better understand him and his message here, you have to know a little about his beliefs first.

Every piece after My Words was given to him by counterparts of himself from different realities throughout the multiverse. This is what medical science has dubbed a mental illness. This is his *Midlife Crisis on Infinite Earths*.

---

[*] The term used here is what is socially acceptable. I consider myself Native American, since I am native to America. Not indigenous mind you but native.